THE NIGHTMARES AND DREAMS OF A BROKEN YOUNG GIRL'S LIFE

EILEEN CORMACK

DEDICATION

I'd like to dedicate this 3rd chapter of my book
to my mother and all those who have lost
someone close to them.

CONTENTS

ACKNOWLEDGEMENTS

This project has truly transformed my life. As I reflect on this journey, I can say with certainty that it has helped me grow into a more positive and compassionate individual. I know that this growth would not have been possible without the unwavering support of some incredible people.

Firstly, my deepest gratitude goes to Marie from W.E.A., Sharon from Future Pathways, and Mary from the Book Whisperer. These wonderful individuals have restored my faith in humanity, showing me that not all the world is harsh or indifferent. Their kindness and support have reminded me that there are compassionate, helpful, and truly caring people out there, dedicated to the well-being of others. To each of you, I say a heartfelt thank you for helping me open the door to this new chapter of my life. Meeting you all has been a blessing, and for that, I am eternally grateful.

When I embarked on this journey, I had no idea where it would lead or how my poems would be received. I can now say, hand on heart, that it has been the most incredible experience of my life. I would also like to give special thanks to the most important person in my life—you have always been by my side, seeing me through the darkest times of these past forty years. You have never judged or criticised me; you simply saw me, Eileen. For that, my love, I am forever thankful. Here's to many more years together. xx

I want to express my gratitude to everyone who purchased the first book in this series. I wasn't sure how it would be received, as it lays my life bare for all to read. There are parts that have been deeply painful, but there are also moments of pure joy. My hope is that these words have brought some comfort to those who are still hurting.

Let's continue...

MOTHER!

I remember that morning,
Looking down upon a face
I no longer recognised,
All drawn in and...
Showing the outline of her once full face,
Hair all gone now.
Just threads which had fallen out of her scarf,
Hands were cold
and lifeless.
I let go of her hand so, I could
tuck her stray hair back under the scarf.

I noticed her hand had stayed
in the same shape as when I held it.
Brown blotches
covered the back of her hands and nails
that had grown,
all twisted and discoloured!

I'm not sure what scared me more,
her nails or her face?
Eyes covered in a cloudy film,
I knew she could no longer see, or hear
my eyes filled with tears,
as they scan down the bed
only to be met with a silhouette,
of the shape of a body.
Fear struck me again,
I knew she had gone,
No movement on the sheet
that covered her fragile body.

LOSS

Her hand in my hand,
So frail, dark and blotchy,
It was cold and so wish I could rub it,
To generate heat from my hand to hers.
Nails all curled up into shapes,
I've never seen before.

Grime lay at the base of those nails.
Why were they not washed? Cleaned?
You couldn't see, it hurt to touch her,
Even the hairs on the back of her hands stood straight up,
and when touched, used to send pain through her tiny body.

Gone were her dark brown tresses,
Just clumps where it hadn't fallen out,
not even a curl to be seen.
As I gaze down the bed where
the body of my mother lay,
her hands getting colder by the minute
and the fear rising within me quicker.

Slipping my hand out from hers,
they stayed in the same shape,
we had created over those few last hours we shared,
I knew she never knew I was there.
The drugs you see,
Comatose by the morphine DF118,
There lay the shell of a once a strong vibrant woman!

Alone I sat ,wishing for an arm to comfort me,
To hold my hand and say ,"it's OK to cry now."

The room took on a strange aura,
Is this what death looked like?
Empty, cold, and so hollow.
As I gaze up at my mother,
her skin so drawn into her face
you could see the structure,
which once was so full and rounded.

Fear takes me as I stumble to get up,
Walking backwards from that bed,
Did I think she was going to sit up?
Yes, I did.
That surreal moment,
A split second thought of her grabbing me.
Closing the door quickly, I stand alone.
Just the door between a mother and a daughter.
I'll never forget that Sunday morning,
A part of me died, gone forever.
Why didn't I ask her why?
Why have you left me?
AGAIN!
Why?
But this time, for keeps,
I'll never know,
No one will,
Only she will know,
why she did what she did
but she's sleeping now,
Rest mum, night night.

I forgive you
xx

THE PRICE PAID!

A face etched with all the pain and wrongs
you had done or gone through,
I see now why you made those choices
You can rest now you have paid the price asked,
The price being the pain you suffered,
before your life was taken from you,
So, rest my mother.
They can't hurt you no-more
And the irony is,
They too had pain for what they had done
So, you are free from them both now
So, rest and sleep tightly mother of mine
And know this, to this day you are loved,
by ME xx

MOTHER HEN

In my life I've always been the mother hen,
Looking after my siblings,
Looking after my mother,
My son,
and even my boyfriends,,

When is it my time?
Time, when someone looks after me,
Loves me for who I am,
and protects me from this oh so
Wicked world,
They say you don't give to receive,
I don't see it like that.

Maybe I cared too much,
Loved too much,
Maybe I'm too intense,
But I can't help that,
I always thought by showing love,
Love would be returned,
Doing his breakfast in bed,
Clothes all nice and clean,
Trying to look nice when he visits.

But it's not so,
I've become their mother,
Doing the things she used to do,
I'm tired now,
Can't chase for love no more,
Can't give no more of myself,
I'm falling again,
Feeling so, so alone!

No friends to talk too,
you all made sure off that,
So alone I sit in these four walls,
wracking my brain what to do next?
But I'm tired of the running after,
cooking the breakfast,
cleaning the house and clothes,
Why did they never cook for me?
Clean for me?
Hug me when I was down!
And give me the cuddle I so desperately needed,
I can't answer those questions,
All I can say is ...
NO MORE!

The wall is up now,
Gotta stop the pain my heart feels,
Love myself more,
Respect myself more,
I'm not their mother,
I'm a person,
A woman with her own needs, desires
Hopes and dreams,

I'm alone again now, nobody calls,
Nobody visits,
I feel nobody cares
About ME!!!
What and where did I go wrong?
Will, someone please tell me,
Am I too needy, loud maybe,
Maybe to fat now,
I'm no longer the slim, sexy woman,

I once was
But I'm old now,
But, Eileen is still here,
Not one of you can see me though, can you.
I know you can't.
Otherwise I would not feel this way.
Lonely, hurt, afraid and most of all.
UNLOVED,
thank you to you all,
For NOTHING!!

YOU REAP WHAT YOU SOW!

Only a baby/child back then,
When the pain started, I mean,
I don't think pain has a number an age,
a preference, it's just,
PAIN!

When you feel it rise within you,
it could just be because,
your cake didn't rise that day
but it will take you back,
to a memory long ago,
maybe you dropped it?
Or ate it cause hunger took you,
Who knows!

But you will remember,
I don't like some cakes now.
Even hate Brussels sprouts,
Sitting at the table being forced fed,
Or told you sit there till all gone,
In my mind
I can still see the sick of those sprouts,
on my top,
And feel the slap that followed.

In my own world,
I say "no child of mine" will go through that,
You know we say that a lot, us lot,
But we made a rod for our own backs,
Spoilt brats, that have no concept of hardship
as mamma works four jobs to give you, what?
What she never had - a hot meal on the table!

13

No sprouts mind,
a smile rises on my face,
a silent laugh,
I wonder...
maybe hardships is not too
much of a bad thing,
In moderation.

It gives you values of how you got
those nice trainers on your feet.
Why you say please and thank you?
My mother always said,
It's cost nothing ... manners,
I can still see her smile,
I can see where and what road I took,
I took the easy road, cry,biscuit,
Moan, bottle, scream, a cuddle,
'You reap what you sow,' people say,
and you do,
You do.

So, mothers I say to you all,
Let them cry, for a bit with no biscuit,
Let them moan for a while for that bottle
when it's time, then give them it,
And if they scream ...
SCREAM BACK

Teach them to care about their mammas,
Teach them love is a two-way street,
and it's better to walk it with a loved one,
wish I had that

LIVING WITH IT!

As I walk through my life in my mind,
I try to remember good times,
Times of laughter, of happiness
And times of joy, but...
Why do I struggle so,
My mind disturbed by the images,
images that take over,
any good memories I may have,
Am I not normal?
Why does my mind wander back to those terrible days?
Days of pain and heartache.

My mangled thoughts
making my body shudder by the thoughts,
that are provoking me,
Taking me to a time where my tears fell,
A time where pain and heartache were all I knew.
Why can't it stop,
Let me have nice thoughts,
Nice memories.

If only I could have been loved,
if only I could have been cared for.
Maybe things could have been different for me
... but they weren't.

SO, I'LL JUST HAVE TO TRY AND LIVE WITH IT!

WHY DID YOU FOLLOW?

They say a damaged heart
can be mended,
I say how can it?
Through love, kindness?
Well, I've tried, and I know
mines can't,
Too messed up,
head swirling,
with all the bad things,
that I've gone through!

People who have hurt me so bad,
it makes my heart twist inside,
And the tears flow,
My insides screaming at me.
Don't forgive them.
You can't forgive them.
Too much badness done,
Too much hurt,
To many tears,
Can't stop the flow.

My thoughts taking me back
to times gone by
time and time again.
Times where I'm shunned,
shunned by my own.
Oh, what short memories they have
They didn't care
It was only me.

Twist the knife deeper then.
'Cause I'll tell you this,
It can't go any deeper,
You all went all the way.
Hand in hand doing me wrong,
Do you all remember?

I know I ain't no saint,
But did I take from youse?
You followed me to here,
Why? Why?

I ran from that city to get away,
To get away from my past,
But you followed,

Why?
WHY ... ?

DAMAGED GOODS

Why can't I find my forever love, Why?
Someone who gets me.
Loves me,
wants me,
Needs me,

To give me that connection I need,.
The firework ,.
Have I no
Spark,
Am I dull,?
Am I too needy?
Do I ask for too much,?
Am I too broken,
To share those surreal moments with you,

Why can't my life be complete,?
HAPPY ,
My forever one beside me
My love,
My partner in crime.
My HUSBAND,.
It's not for you,
I hear my mind saying,
Not for you,
Your damaged goods,
so, forget those dreams,
Forget your needs,
I've got you
Pain says,!!!
You are mine!!!

A GIFT

I remember that morning
as if it was yesterday,
Laid across my chest ...
Still wet, eyes wide open, and crying to be fed.
As my eyes passed over his body,
All fingers and toes accounted for,
Perfect to me in every way,
I realised what a gift I was given,
My tears welling up,
I plant a gentle kiss upon his forehead,
Thank you God I say, thank you,

He's a man now,
independent and full of compassion,
for his fellow man,
Strong and tall he stands before me,
As I look up, I see the glistening in his eyes,
and his bright white teeth smiling back at me.
He's a quiet man,
Not afraid of his own company,
His gentle ways empowering him,
Allowing others to feel safe,
safe in his gentle ways and strong heart,
He's never been a bother,
There for me at every turn,
Or to catch me when I fall.

I've fallen many times throughout his life,
But never has he judged me for it,
You see he's a survivor like me,
Surviving the wrongs done to him,

Surviving his own trials in life,
A life that's been full of obstacles, but, once again
All taken in his stride...
An inner peace glows from his face
and his faith holding him strong when times get tough,
You see... that's my son,
My gentle man ,
A gift that was given me,
I thank you Jehovah,
I thank you....!

IT'S ONLY PAIN

Sleep evades me,
It hides itself in the crevices of my inner mind,
saying you don't need it.
You don't need it,
Stay awake so those hands can't touch,
Break you once more.
But it's not those hands that stops my sleep this time,
It's the PAIN.

The pain that engulfs me to my very core,
My eyes red and blotchy from the night's tears,
Tears that ran like the Nile.
Long and fast tearing up my face,
as I wipe them away with the corner of my nightie.

Can't take this pain no more
they say they put dogs down if they're in pain,
Put me down, put me down.
Feet stinging like walking on thistles.
Legs burning like the mid-day sun,
Knees twisting up like a car crusher,
The dull nagging pain
shooting arrows down my arms,
leaving from my fingertips.

Shall I go on?
About the pain that is.
I'm so bored of this constant pain,
no days off, just overtime,
when I'm supposed to be asleep?

No wages for that,
Just eyes that burn like fire and a body... broken!

Not through my past, but by my NOW!
let me rest you wicked thing,
How could you hurt someone so much,
Maybe I should just shack up with the crack
Take my body elsewhere,
Drink to oblivion,
and maybe scream in the streets,
I know I can't do these things,
I WON'T do these things,
But I'm running out of options here.

I fear.
I fear how far this pain will take me,
It will make me or break me,
I'm stuck only with 2 choices,
Crap world ain't it,
Then I remember,
Only a few hours more,
I'll be fine. I'll be OK,
I'll be sleeping once more,
Watching the clock,
Time, tick tock. tick tock, don't stop,
Trying to write these words,
all merging together,
But I won't stop,
I won't stop,
I ain't going back,
All will be fab,
When I get me jab,
We will talk to you again Eileen,
to you again,

Tick tock,tick tock

But I'm not a dog, you can't put me down,
I've got an agenda,
Places to go,
People to meet, and yes ,maybe even greet,
You're a lion with your mane,
and a warrior with a name,
You are a WARRIOR now,
No pain, no GAIN,
So don't get on that fast train out of here,
You can get through this Eileen
.... it's only pain!!

A BED OF ROSES!

What is happiness really like?
Is it like, a bed of roses,
is it full of joy?
Or is it the home,
that keeps you all safe and warm,
Maybe its laugher,
Maybe it's knowing you're loved,
Maybe it's all your friends that
make you laugh each day,
Maybe it's that feeling of a full belly,
Or even the blanket that keeps you warm,
Never to worry about your next meal,
Never to worry
you're wearing the wrong clothes,
Never having to worry
that, that beating won't come,
Is that what happiness is?

Mmmm,
I wouldn't know,
if it slapped me across my face,
even if it introduced itself to me,
Cause you see,
I don't believe in happiness,
It's a myth,
A dream one has,
An escape one needs,
A desire we crave for.

I'm that used to feeling, miserable,
I should have been named that,

I would have had an excuse then,
for the empty belly,
The slaps across my face,
The cold that hurt my bones
The clothes that got
me beat every day,
The friends I couldn't have,
The friends I never had,
So, you see,
I don't know what it's like to be happy,
I only know.
I want to die!!

WHY DID YOU HURT ME?

You didn't see me,
But I saw you,
You didn't feel me,
But I felt you,
Why I ask why?
I did you no wrong,
I never hurt you,
Why did you hurt me so?
Is it cause she left?
Is it because I was hers?
Or was it control?

Yes, you controlled me,
Beat me.
Denied me.
You denied me,
my human right!
To be loved
To be cared for
To feel wanted
But I wasn't, was I?

You just needed a babysitter.
A punch bag,
to verbally abuse!
Dehumanising me ...
Making me feel dirty,
I was just a product of her,
You said, and funnily enough
you did try and say sorry,
Oh, but not by yourself ... oh no,

Not YOU!
Through others,
You had to go through the nurses
that cared for you.
Well, all I can say
I wasn't interested then
and not now.

Too late now anyway,
You should have told me yourself,
but
YOU'RE DEAD
NOW!

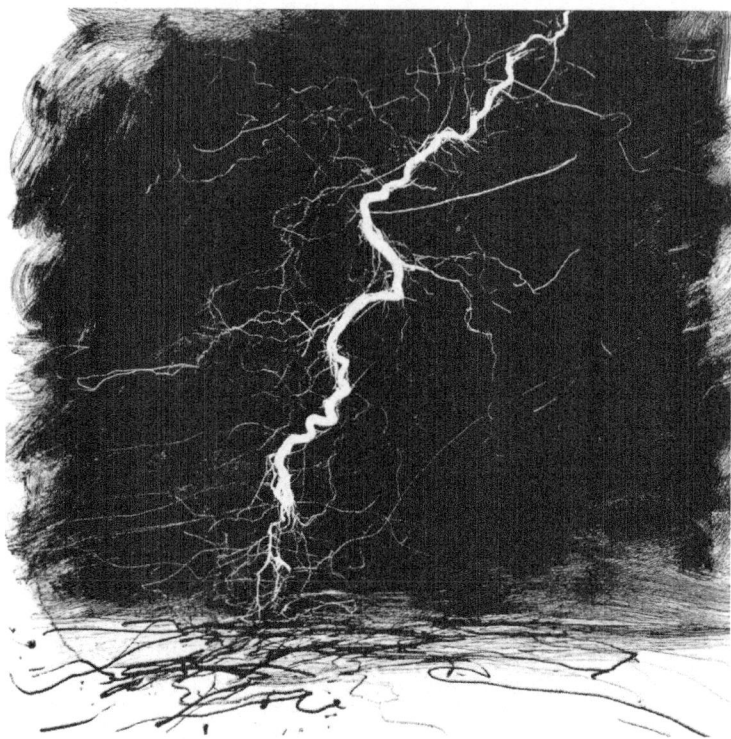

SHOCKS!

Pain has come once again to visit me.
Wracking my body with shocks
that perpetuate the pain that my body feels,
Electric shocks surges throughout my body
twisting my face into shapes,
that I'm glad I don't see.

I feel the water dribbling out
from the side of my mouth
not able to close or wipe
as my brain is trying what to do first,
rub my knees that are screaming at me
my back which with every move makes
contorts my face further
Pain has got me,
by the 'short and curlies'
you could say.

A state of confusion takes over me,
What do I do?
What can I do?
More meds?
Cut myself?
I just don't know,

Confusion has clouded my thoughts
I don't know anymore,
I just want it to end
a life with no pain,
what a dream,
But that's all it is a dream,

I can't write no more,
My mind,
fingers dead,
no more thoughts.
I just want to die
Don't wake me,
up body of mine,
Let me go,
I've had enough now!

THE BOYFRIEND

If I could count all the times,
you hurt me,
I'd get lost in time,
The times you cheated,
The times you lied,
The times you hid,
behind that big door.
The list is endless,
like my love was.

But you destroyed that
time and time again,
I forgave your wrongs,
Time and time again
I took you back,
What for?
For you to hurt me again.
And again, and again!

Well I've woke up now,
I can see,
straight through your selfish ways,
All about your needs,
YOUR wants!
YOUR desires!
YOUR silence!
I was lost to a computer.

A game,
the lads,
never gave me time,

Time to talk,
Time to cuddle...
Time to share a kiss...
Time to share those oh so,
special moments,
I was alone when we were together,
Alone in the silence
of a movie you were watching.

Alone in the silence,
of a game you were playing,
A computer widow I became,
A widow in every way...
Alone,
in the silence
of your kind of love,
Well, I broke that silence,
I broke from your selfishness,
I broke from your ignorance
I broke away from your neglect!

You broke my heart
BUT,
I'll tell you something,
I'm fine now...
I know now I wasted those years,
Waiting for my love to be returned,
My love to be valued,
My body to be held,
To feel safe,
Needed,
Wanted!

What for I ask myself,

I'll tell you ,
For NOTHING...
Cause you gave me...nothing...
Not love,
Not a cuddle,
Not your heart...
Nothing...
BUT PAIN!!

LOVE?

When you've never had it,
what does that mean???
My friends say,
It's a warm feeling in your tummy
And butterflies flutter away in your heart,.
The warm arms around you,
protecting you,making you feel safe,
They say it's a hard thing to describe,
But you will know when you feel it,
I've never had those arms around me,
my heart fluttering like a butterfly,
feeling safe and warm,
Why is that?
I think I'm unlovable,
cause...
I'm damaged goods?,

A BROKEN HEART

You broke my heart
You stole my very being,
You stole my soul,
You stole ME!!
Why did you all do that?
You left behind your sniggers,
someone broken,
Feeling nothing,
Unable to love,
Unable to feel,
All you left were the tears,
The tears that run like a burn,cold ,oh so cold,
A heart burnt by the pain you inflicted,
You all left me with nothing,
A nobody,
Empty inside,
Feeling nothing, but the tears on my face,

Year in and year out,
All the same,
Why can't I change the record,
Sing a song of happiness.
A song of love and cuddles...
why can't I feel the warmth,
of a cup of hot chocolate in my mug ,
Warming my insides as it goes down,
I'll tell you why,
Cause it's not real,
Only dreams that I once dreamt of,
Happiness I wished for
But did not get.

The cuddle I yearned for,
or the warm touch of someone's hand
saying it will be alright,
I got yah,
I gotcha,
I've stopped wishing now,
I just need the nightmares to stop,
And then I'll be ok,
Or will I?

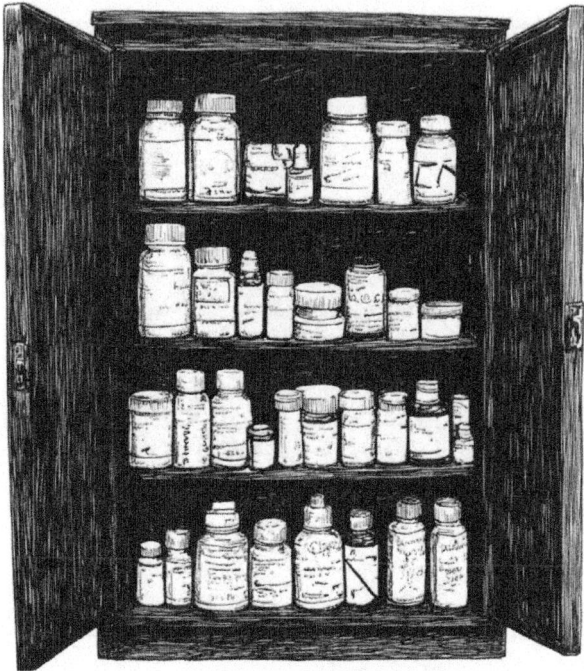

MY PAIN

I hate you sleep!
Night after night
I try but you won't let me.
Nightmares engulf me
filling my head with memories,
of times gone by,
Memories that tore into my very soul,
Pain takes over when your nightmare is there
racking my body with shock after shock,
the electricity ravages me.
I can feel that pain,
Night after night waking me
I'm hurting.

My body feeling like it's being ripped apart,
Tablet after tablet I take,
Hoping this tablet,
will be the one to make it stop,
But it doesn't.
Relentlessly hurting me,
I ask myself which is worse?
The pain that torments me,
on every nerve in my body,
twisting them , trying to make me scream.
Or is it the nightmares of YOU
tearing at my body in a different way,
through my memories,
I can't decide,
All I know is,
I hate you,
Cause you both hurt me!

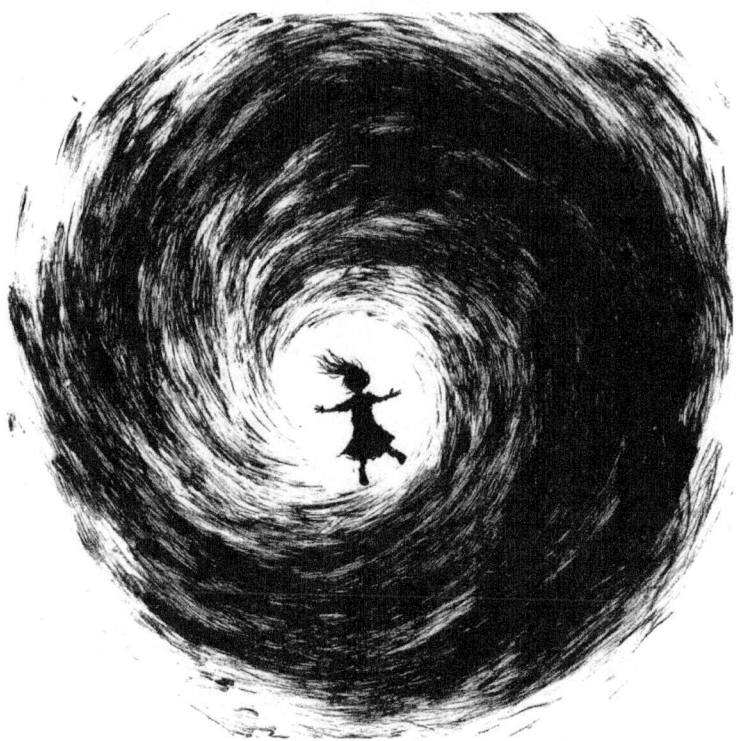

SUCKED IN!

Do you know what it feels like
not wanting to be here?
Alive on this planet
a planet full of so many beautiful things
and people.
Do you know what it feels like
to want the world to devour you...
Erase your name from its vaults which hold it
erase you like a rubber on a piece of paper
Rubbing out a mistake!
Well, I do...
I feel like a mistake
feeling like I should never have been born...
Wanting my name erased from ever existing.

Death doesn't fear me
I welcome it...
I want it...
The pain will stop you see.
The pain of my past
A past that ripped me up and threw me away
Rubbed my face in the dirt, constantly.

My body twisting each time I walk, sit, bend.
So why should I want to live?
Why should I?
I see the pretty flowers
In full bloom
I feel the grass between my toes
I feel the sun beating down on me, but,
I still don't like it here.

It's a cold and lonely place.
This place called earth.
Especially if your face don't fit,
mine's never did!

You see I feel I was a glitch,
a freak of nature,
a blot on the landscape.
I'm waiting,
for the rubber to rub me away

Please come soon
please come
I've had enough now
enough pain
enough hurt
enough sorrow
So take me
to that hole in the ground
cover me over
... no sign of who I am
or was.

Thank you.

HEAVY

Sitting in this chair,
I feel heavy. Oh, so heavy,
Life didn't cut me no breaks in my life,
and every day the pain of my past,
shows its ugly head, once more.

You know, I said to a friend,
When does this stop,
When does life for me become easy,
or even just plain easier,
'Lol,' I laugh to myself,
the tears mingling with the snotty nose
no tissue, so your sleeve ends up suffice!

Are we marked when we're born?
Are we born to suffer? To feel pain.
To feel the hurt,
day by day
a relentless fear of what's to come next!
Is this life's big plan,
Is this what makes us unique individuals??
How can it be so,
child after child
carrying the burden of their years.

Pain has no age limit you know
whether you're 1, 2, 3 or 23,
when that pain comes, it changes you
some become bitter, angry
some hide behind the closed curtains,
hiding from their shame.

Is it my fault?
Why doesn't someone come?
Why don't people see what's being done?
"Nah, none of ma busines,s" I hear,
"Stay away," I hear,
if only ONE had spoken.
I WOULD NOT be writing these words!

So, I say, shame on you,
you on-lookers
shame on you,
none of my 'business people'
shame on you,
you curtain twitchers
shame,
SHAME!

Cause I was only a child,
I didn't cause the shame,
All I needed
was somebody to help me,
BUT nobody came,
not even the curtain twitchers!!!!

A JUMBLE OF DREAMS

When things get dark and your mind clouds up,
just try and remember who or what took you there.
Who caused this darkness that makes you unable to sleep,
tossing and turning throughout the night,
night terrors I call them!

Dreams that are a jumble of events,
that don't make sense, but they still frighten you...
A mixture of the past and the present
making their own story in that dreamland...
Taking you back to an old home maybe,
but the wrong people are there.

As you walk through the nightmare
people from the past
talking, shouting,
you start to run faster and faster,
just get to the door my mind says,
but it's evading me...
Like a dark tunnel,
getting further and further away.

Suddenly, a voice shouts
I'm in another room,
chattering people,
the music getting louder and louder.
Why am I back here?
Back in that room of terror,
cowering in the corner,
not daring to move!

A feeling of warmth
touches my leg first,
then my feet
looking down I see the water
flowing out of me
winding its way down
it's getting wider and faster
it's rising!

I'm trapped,
higher and higher the water,
is engulfing me,
screaming...
"Help me someone, help me
I'm drowning, give me your hand,
pull me out, don't let me drown".

A hand grabs me...
Gasping for breath,
my eyes open
where am I now...?
am I awake?
Fear enters my mind once again...
not sure if I'm in the present or the past.

My eyes darting around the room,
looking for something familiar
my heart pounding against my chest,
as if it's trying to escape out of my body.
Sweat pouring down my forehead
hands clammy and oh so hot,
I lie there
And wait ...

Wait for my heart to slow down,
and the heat of my body,
to return to normal
I'm awake

Tears well up in my eyes.
Why do I dream so, why?
Why can't I rest like a normal person?
No dreams evoking my inner thoughts...
Playing with them,
jumbling up,
time,
space,
events.

Just let me sleep
like normal people
But I'm not normal
AM I !!!
From what?
Reliving the terror,
of a past you want to forget...!

SWITCHED OFF!

Laying there,alone in my bed
I wonder,
How's it come to this,
Struggling with my inner thoughts
that are playing
ticktacktoe with my brain
Why this? Why that?
I wonder this
and wonder that,
I wish I could winter my mind.
Put it to sleep,
even for just an hour.

My brain playing tricks on me
fooling me into believing in me
It's just a horrible joke
A cruel, cruel joke.
I'm unable to focus
think,
work things out,
what's going on!
Am I losing it?

Whatever it is,
We should have a switch,
To turn ourselves off
when we've had enough,
Even just for a rest,
I'd love one,
I'd switch myself off
permanently!!!!!!

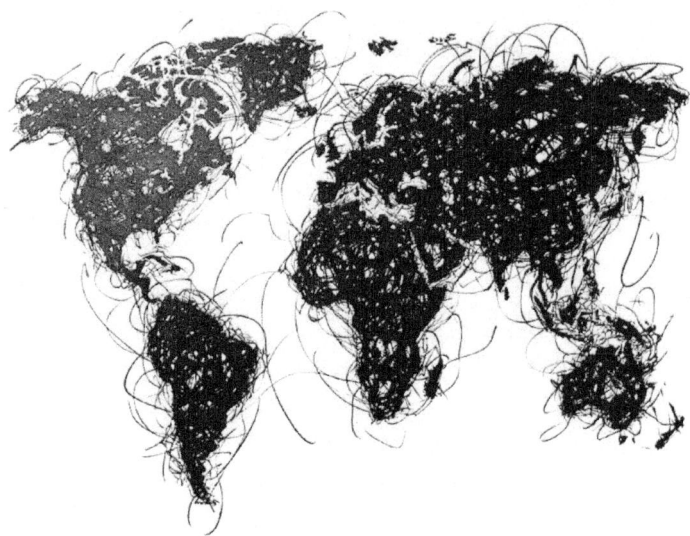

THE MAP OF LIFE

When I ask myself….
Why me? Why me?
Was I chosen to be hurt,
beaten,
shamed,
throughout my life,
was this my so-called destiny
if you believe in that!

Was my life already mapped out for me?
Or was I just one of the unlucky ones
the one who would take the pain,
take the sorrow and the shame,
that followed.
All the blows that rained down on me,
or the boot that used to catch my head,
as I ducked.

Or was it running the gauntlet?
Ducking and diving from that clenched fist
Why me? Why me?
Maybe it was because if I took it in my life,
Some other child would be safe.
Maybe I was supposed to have this life so
I'd take their blows,
their sorrow and their pain.

All I do know is, if that's true
I'm glad I had the life I did
cause that other little girl,
might not have survived

the blows,
the pain...
the mental nightmare of my life!

So, I'm glad it was me and not you,
Cause I survived that pain,
made myself humble to that sorrow,
I'm alright now,
life is holding my hand,
and walking with me,
I hope you are happy little girl,

Safely tucked up in your bed,
no boogiemen to scare you,
Just a life full of fun and laughter
I survived, so I'm OK now,
Night night, wee lassie...
.... night night!

FAIRYTALES

Be careful of what you wish for,
the old saying goes
but I wish I'd had a wish
I'd wish I'd never been born,
I'd wish for the beating to stop.

I'd wish for the wicked people
in my life to be gone!
But I know it's only a fairy tale,
a made-up saying
was it to give us hope?
Or to dream of better things,
A better life maybe?
A life without pain
a life without misery
or memories from the past,
a past that defined us.

Well, me I'd just keep on wishing the same wish
I wish I'd never been born!
Born into a life where I was
used and abused,
A life where pain was my only comforter
at least I could concentrate on that
I never understood why I came into this world.

I suppose many of us don't,
The pain we endure,
day after day,
Making its mark with every whip,
punch, slap, or kick.

So, there's no point in wishing,
Wishing won't make it stop,
Wishing won't make it go away,
Wishing they were dead,
our abusers I mean,
So take it all on the chin,
soak it up,
every slap,
punch and kick.

You will hear "You deserved that!"
Or...
"Why do you make me hurt you?"
"You're a wicked person, I'll beat it out of you!"
All I say is,
There will come a time
a time when the years have passed,
when you're bigger,
older,
wiser,
you will be able
to fight back
kick back
slap back
or WALK
even run away!
Me, I got a train
a one-way ticket out of there!

Said I'd never go back,
walk those streets again,
But I did
and I'm glad I did

because I was wiser
older
and I could fight back now,
So don't dream of wishes
dream of years to come
you will get there
you will buy that bus ticket

Maybe even a plane
or train ticket out of there,
So just dream for now
just dream,
It's those dreams that keep you going,
I now,
Because I dreamt that dream,
And look at me now!
I'm standing tall,
Making my own way in this world
a world where no body
will ever beat me,
hit me…. again
without me hitting back !!!.

BRIDGES!

For all the bridges,
I've crossed,
walked over
ran from.
I can see you all now.

No matter how tall that bridge,
I'll climb you,
for all the bridges broken,
I'll fix you...
For all the bridges,
I've crossed,
I won't again.

You see,
no matter how high,
How broken,
How long,
I've conquered them all.

So, I don't need
to be frightened no more,
I can walk on the road around you,
I don't need to cross you,
I'll take the bus, taxi, train.
Cause I know
there are other ways to go....
And I'll go my own way now!

Printed in Great Britain
by Amazon

49480306R00050